T0005883

A DAY IN THE LIFE
Bugs

WHAT DO BEES, ANTS, AND DRAGONFLIES GET UP TO ALL DAY?

NEON  SQUID

Contents

Welcome to the world of bugs!

I've always loved insects. Who wouldn't be fascinated, when swimming or fishing at a lake, by the amazing variety of colors, shapes, and sizes of dragonflies flying by? Now, as a scientist working at the **American Museum of Natural History** in New York, I spend my days studying dragonflies, damselflies, termites, cockroaches, and other insects.

As an **entomologist**—that means someone who studies bugs—I travel the world to observe insects in their natural habitats, whether that's in the cold tundra of the Arctic or in hot tropical rainforests near the equator. There are over **one million species of insects** and so many more waiting to be discovered! Some insects are predators, hunting other insects for food, while other insects are prey, with strategies to escape predators. The world of insects is full of competition and cooperation, feast and famine, tenacity and timidness.

Studying insects up close has shown us that their days are filled with adventure—from early morning to late into the night. In this book, we will follow the journeys of insects throughout a full day and observe what they're up to!

Dr. Jessica L. Ware

A dragonfly basks in the sun

By the side of a pond in North America, a **green darner dragonfly** is starting its day. Gripped tightly to a reed, it has wings that are covered in dew. As the sun rises, the dragonfly begins to warm, whirring its wings to shake off any remaining water. Gradually, its color shifts from dark purple to bright blue. The dragonfly beats its wings and **takes flight**, zipping over the pond in search of something to eat for breakfast.

Ahead, some flies hover over a lily pad, and the hungry dragonfly heads in that direction. But then there's a sudden splash—leaping from the water is a **frog!** Its sticky tongue shoots toward the dragonfly. The dragonfly darts to the left, then cuts to the right, to escape the frog's clutches. The frog flops back into the water. Better luck next time!

A trap is set...

When they grow up, antlions get wings.

An ant wanders slowly over sandy soil in North Africa, unaware of the **grave danger** it's in. As the ant walks, the rising sun casts its shadow along the edge of a deep sandy pit.

Below, barely poking out of the bottom of the pit, hides a young **antlion**—an insect famous for hunting ants. With its mouth wide open, the antlion's legs wiggle in anticipation. One wrong step from the ant and breakfast will be served! The ant plods along, and then, too close to the edge, it slips and begins to slide. The antlion starts flinging sand at the ant, making it harder for it to climb back up.

Eventually the antlion snaps its jaws and clasps the ant, enjoying its meal. After a few minutes the ant has been consumed. The antlion then sets the trap for the next meal—**lunch!**

Meanwhile...
After a year spent underwater eating as much as he could, a mayfly emerges at the surface as an adult. His wings unfurl, and he sets off in search of a mate!

The cocoon breaks open

In the jungles of Madagascar, off the coast of mainland Africa, a female comet moth pushes out of a cocoon to meet the world. A few months ago she was a caterpillar, chomping her way through lots of leaves. Then she spun a silk cocoon from a branch and curled up inside, ready to begin a dramatic transformation into her adult form. This process is called **metamorphosis**.

As the comet moth emerges, her brand-new wings are weak and damp. She grips tightly to the outer surface of the cocoon as she dries, allowing her wings to get sturdier and ready for flight. The sun warms her, and she slowly flaps her wings to test them out. She has spent most of her life as a caterpillar and has only a few days as an adult. Her goal is to find a male that she can mate with. But the jungle is **full of dangers**, so this comet moth better stay alert...

As a caterpillar the comet moth had one job—eat as much as possible!

The cocoon has holes in it, possibly to help water drain out when it's raining.

After three months in
the cocoon, the adult
female emerges.

Winged wonders

Some wings are small and some are many times the size of the insect's body. Insects use their wings in all sorts of cool and different ways—including to fly, to communicate, and to help them hide.

Glass wings

A dragonfly's wings are transparent, or see-through, but the many wing veins make them sturdy—perfect for fast flight.

Back off!

This praying mantis has hind wings with big black markings on them. As the wings unfurl, the mantis seems bigger, startling predators with a message to leave it alone!

Hide-and-seek

Is that leaf moving? A leaf insect's wings look so much like a leaf that it is almost impossible to spot!

Make some noise

Crickets make their distinctive chirp by rubbing one wing across another. This is called stridulation.

Masterpiece

Like stained glass, this arctiid moth's wings have slivers of color in an intricate pattern that resembles a work of art.

Giant wings

Some insects, such as atlas moths, have wings that dwarf their actual bodies.

Armor

A beetle's hind wings are thin and designed for flight, but its forewings form something called the elytra. The elytra is tough and protects the hind wings when the beetle crawls under bark and soil.

Time to fly

After spending their youth underground, future queen ants use their wings for the first time to try to find a mate.

After a hard morning's work, the honeybees gather

WAGGLE WAGGLE!

WAGGLE WAGGLE!

Flying back to the hive, a honeybee is excited to tell her sisters about the patch of flowers she has found out past the lake. When she enters the hive, she begins to **dance!** But she's not just dancing for fun—contained in her funky moves is a secret message.

Bees search for flowers they can forage for **nectar** and **pollen**, which they bring back to the colony and use to make honey. After finding a good patch of flowers, bees fly back to the hive and perform a **"waggle dance"** to communicate the direction and distance to the flower patch. This way, their sisters can easily find the same flowers and help collect nectar and pollen.

During the dance, the honeybee moves her body in a certain direction, which tells her sisters what **angle** they need to fly away from the sun to get to the flower patch. The **distance** she moves in the dance shows the bees how far away the flower patch is. If the patch is close to the hive, she will dance in a circle. Her sisters watch carefully, memorize the directions, and then set off!

All of the bees in a colony are sisters, and their mother is the queen.

Orchid mantises
are a type of
praying mantis.

Mantis standoff!

Deep in the forests of Indonesia, in Southeast Asia, an **orchid mantis** is as still as a statue. He perfectly blends into his surroundings—his pink-and-white legs, head, and body look just like a flower. Suddenly, the stem of the plant the mantis is on starts to sway. Another orchid mantis is climbing up the stalk! Within seconds, the mantises are face-to-face: two predators ready to fight each other.

The first mantis quickly lifts up his forelegs and stands with his other legs spread. He stretches out his wings and turns to directly face the newly arrived mantis.

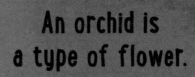

An orchid is
a type of flower.

Meanwhile... Brightly colored
shield bugs stand out against the
green leaves they're feeding on.
The colors signal to predators
(such as birds) that the bugs taste
bad and should be avoided!

Soon, both mantises are swaying side to side,
their arms raised and **wings outstretched**.
Each mantis attempts to appear larger and more
intimidating than the other. The first mantis steps
forward toward his challenger. The newly arrived
mantis considers his options before backing away,
folding his wings over his abdomen. He scurries

Marching ants

One after another, worker leaf-cutter ants march along a branch in a rainforest in the heart of South America. Further along, two workers are clipping pieces of leaves from small plants with their mouthparts, or **mandibles**, and dropping them in a pile.

Other ants arrive at the pile. They pick up the leaf pieces and venture off along the branch in the direction of the ant nest. These ants have super strength—they're capable of carrying leaves many times their own weight.

The sun is hot above, and the ants walk quickly, laying down smells called **pheromone scents** to make the path easy to recognize for the other ants. Arriving at the entrance to the nest, an ant pushes through the muddy opening and, in darkness, trudges through a tunnel to place its piece of leaf on a large pile. The leaf pieces will be sorted and transported to a **fungus garden** deep within the nest.

The cicadas emerge...

Periodical cicadas emerge every 13 or 17 years.

In the eastern United States, a periodical cicada nymph emerges from the muddy soil at the base of a tree trunk, and it's not alone... Trillions of its siblings are also emerging in scenes resembling a **zombie apocalypse**. The cicada nymph blinks in the sunlight—not surprising, since it's been underground for 17 years! Crawling up the trunk, gripping the bark with its sharp claws, the nymph forces its skin to open, allowing the adult cicada to climb out. It leaves its shed skin still attached to the tree. The adult clings to the trunk, its small red eyes and red wing veins standing out against the brown tree bark. Suddenly a **blue jay** swoops down to the tree and helps itself to a beakful of bugs that are taking flight. There's danger everywhere, but by emerging in their trillions the cicadas give themselves a better chance of surviving. Today our cicada friend avoided being eaten by the luck of the draw.

Whirligig beetles

Whirligig beetles swim in circles on the surface of the pond. They look above water with the top halves of their eyes and underwater with the bottom halves!

Super swimmers

If you look closely at a pond, you'll observe plenty of insects going about their business. While some beetles twirl along on the surface, others dive deep into the pond in search of food.

Pond skaters

Ultralight pond skaters can literally walk on water. The water's surface forms a very thin skin that they can glide along.

Diving beetle

Diving beetles have long hind legs covered in hairs. These legs push them forward underwater as they try to catch tadpoles for dinner. They carry an air bubble to help them breathe.

Some insects can breathe underwater.

Giant water bugs

Male giant water bugs carry their future children as they swim. Dozens of eggs are arranged in neat rows on their backs.

Water scorpions

Water scorpions aren't actually scorpions, they just look like them. They're spindly bugs, and they can't swim very well!

The hunt is on

The green darner dragonfly soars in the air, gliding on a warm breeze. It has a big journey coming up, and it needs to eat to build up its fat stores. It will use this fat as energy when it sets off on its long-distance flight, or **migration**. A butterfly flutters by, dancing low above a pretty meadow. The dragonfly isn't admiring the scene though. It senses an opportunity...

Dragonflies
can move each
of their four wings
separately for
maximum control.

The dragonfly gets the butterfly in its sights and narrows in on its prey. It swoops down and quickly clasps the butterfly with its spiny legs. The dragonfly brings the butterfly toward its **mandibles** and starts chewing on its juicy, fatty abdomen mid-flight. The dragonfly lands on a branch, still clasping the butterfly, and quickly bites off the wings, dropping them to the ground. The meal is over in mere minutes. Then, not wasting a second, the dragonfly takes off into the air again in search of more nourishment.

Hatching eggs

A shield bug crouches low on a branch, protecting something very special. Beneath her abdomen, eggs are attached to the branch in **neat, organized rows**. From the blue sky above, the eggs can barely be seen. The shield bug mom's body hides them from sight.

Suddenly the shield bug senses movement beneath her. She moves aside as a small hole appears in one of the eggs, then another, and then another. Soon, small, jewel-like **nymphs** are climbing out of their eggs, eating the egg shells as their first meals!

Mom's work is now done, so she heads off. The shield bug nymphs stay near the half-eaten egg shells in a tight formation, or **aggregation**. It's safer for them to stick together. The nymphs look like adult shield bugs, just smaller. In the next few weeks they will shed their skin, or molt, several times as they grow to their adult size.

Meanwhile... Two male cicadas are singing by vibrating their tymbals, a thin layer on their abdomens. It's hot, and singing takes a lot of energy. A female hears them and flies over, approaching the male with the loudest, longest song notes.

Can you spot the mantis?

Hide-and-seek

The sun is beginning to drop lower in the sky, and the orchid mantis is hungry. Soon night will fall, and the time for hunting small insects will cease. The mantis stretches out his **raptorial forelegs**, which he uses for grasping prey. These legs are covered in tiny spines, making them formidable weapons. The mantis is hidden in plain sight—his pink-and-white coloring makes him look like orchid flower petals moving in the breeze.

With a flourish, a **hoverfly** speeds in and lands on the flower, looking for nectar. Its speedy landing causes the flower to sway from side to side. For the orchid mantis, dinner has just been delivered! He waits, still as a statue, for just a moment. Then he snaps his forelegs on the fly, giving it no chance of escape. Satisfied, the mantis brings his bent forelegs toward the mandibles in his mouth. The hoverfly will make a perfect afternoon snack.

Hitchhikers

Many insects and arachnids (members of the spider family) hitch a ride on other animals to go from A to B. Others use birds, reptiles, mammals, and other insects as their home, living on them full-time!

Pseudoscorpions

Pseudoscorpions are arachnids that look like little scorpions. Some of them live on ground beetles, where they hunt mites that also make the beetles their home.

Mites

This dragonfly is covered by small red pearls. They look pretty, but they're actually small mites—parasites that feed on the dragonfly.

A parasite is an animal that lives in or on another animal, growing at the expense of its host.

Lice

This blue jay's feathers are speckled with dark dots: lice! The female lice cling to feathers, where they lay their eggs. The lice can't survive for long without their host.

Fleas

If you see a cat scratching, it may have fleas. The fleas hop around among the fur. They use piercing and sucking mouthparts to drink the cat's blood.

The fungus farm

All of the leaf-cutter ants in the nest are **sisters**, but they don't all have the same job. Some of them work in the fungus garden. Their job is to move leaf cuttings that have been brought in by the foragers to different parts of the garden. By doing this, they're feeding the fungus that grows there. These sisters ensure that there is enough fungus for the ants in the colony to eat. And no ant is more important than their mother, the **queen ant**.

One ant moves her feelers, or antennae, along the fungus and notices something is wrong. There is bacteria growing in a patch of the garden—and it's not supposed to be there!

She uses her mandibles to remove the infected section and carries it to an **underground dump** deep below the colony. As she walks, she passes some of her sisters who are feeding baby ants (larvae) with recently harvested fungus. Everyone in the nest has a job to do—all together they make an awesome team.

The dance of the mayflies

The mayfly has a short window of time to find a mate: less than a week! He has spent his life as a nymph underwater, eating and growing. But now he emerges and takes to the skies in a swarm of other mayflies—and they're all **looking for love**.

He flutters along a couple of feet above the water. The air above the lake is thick with small gnats and other mayflies. Occasionally a large dragonfly flies through the crowd, eating a mayfly for its dinner. There is strength in numbers, and our friend the mayfly escapes being eaten!

To his left and right, mayflies who have paired up descend to the water to join together and lay eggs for the next summer's generation of mayflies. Our mayfly keeps flapping his wings, using energy he has stored in his body over the previous months as a nymph. His wings are flimsy, and he moves unsteadily through the swarm. Suddenly, when it looks as if all hope is lost, he **bumps into a female**. They clasp each other with their legs, thankful that they have found each other at last.

Mayflies have a distinctive dancing flight. They fly upward before parachuting down. Then they repeat!

Bee vision

The honeybee buzzes along, flapping her wings and soaring through the summer evening breeze. The sun sits low in the sky above the horizon, its light reflecting off the **flowers in the field** below.

To an average human, the field of flowers would seem like a mixture of brightly colored petals. However, as she swoops down over the meadow. the honeybee can see additional patterns on the flower petals. This is because she can see **ultraviolet light**, as well as blue and green colors.

The patterns on the flowers give the honeybee clues as to which ones have the sweetest nectar. She's able to identify the different flowers even when flying at high speed because she sees things five times faster than humans can. As well as her eyes, she uses special light-sensing organs, called **ocelli**, to survey the meadow. Finally she chooses a flower and lands, ready to drink!

Buzzzzzzzzzzzz

Human vision

Buzzzzzzzzzzzzz

Buzzzzzzzzzzzzzzzzzzzzzzz

Bee vision

Buzzzzzzzzzzzzzzzzzzzzzzzz

City bugs

If you think insects only live in rural areas, think again. Bugs like the urban lifestyle as much as anyone, and living in close proximity to humans can provide some benefits.

Moths

Moths use the light of the moon to navigate at night. However, they can't distinguish moonlight from electric light, which is why you see them fluttering around streetlights.

Cockroaches

There's nothing cockroaches like more than the sight of a trash can. They will quickly climb it and use their mandibles to feast on old chips.

Ants

If one ant knows about a trash can, they all do. Working together, they collect food to take back to the colony.

Bees

Where there's nectar, you'll find bees. City gardens, balconies, and even window boxes make perfect feeding spots.

Wasps

You should always throw used cans in the recycling bin. If you don't, you can be sure they will be visited by wasps—they love sugar!

Ladybugs

City trees are home to lots of bugs. Ladybugs will climb up the rough tree bark toward the tree canopy, where they will rest overnight.

Crickets

It may not be a piece of grass swaying in the wind, but a fence railing provides a good vantage spot for a cricket. Here it can sing in the hopes of attracting a mate.

A journey begins

The green darner dragonfly soars over a sandy beach, snacking on a quick meal of flies that will ensure it has lots of energy. And it will need it—this dragonfly is about to embark on an epic **migration**. This journey will take it hundreds of miles to somewhere warmer where it can lay its eggs.

The dragonfly soars out over the ocean, rising to a spot high enough above the waves to avoid getting salt water on its wings. It flies to the south, staying close to the coastline. The warm wind pushes the dragonfly along, allowing it to glide and soar, conserving energy. Few birds and bats are out over the ocean this evening. The dragonfly is joined on the migration by dozens of other dragonflies; hopefully there is strength in numbers and they can make it safely to their destination.

Meanwhile... The female mayfly rests on the surface of the water, her legs outstretched, and begins to lays her eggs. The small, hard ovals quickly sink to the bottom.

The dragonflies will occasionally stop to rest on vegetation and eat more insects.

The night lights up

Night has fallen, and the sky is dark. A firefly moves through the warm summer air, darting through a quiet forest. She lands on a log and scans the sky for **flashing lights**. She doesn't have to wait long. Within a couple of minutes, the darkness above her erupts into a firework display of golden light!

The twinkling lights come from the abdomens of other fireflies in the sky. They're not all the same species. Each type of firefly has its own pattern of flashing lights, so she needs to pay attention to the **frequency of flashes** being made by the males in the sky above.

Suddenly, she sees what she was looking for: two flashes, a long pause, and then another two flashes! She quickly responds, a **chemical reaction** in her abdomen creating a glowing light signal of her own. She's sending a message to the male above that she is the same species. He flies down to meet her. She has found a mate!

10PM The comet moth flies in the night

Flapping her wings, the comet moth launches herself out into the night sky. But she's not alone...

A **hungry bat** is on the hunt. Luckily, the comet moth has a trick up her sleeve. Moths in the comet moth's family have two pairs of wings, and the hind pair look like two long tails. As she flies, the comet moth twirls the ends of her **hind wings**.

The **twirling wings** affect the echo system the bat uses to hunt. Thinking the hind wings are a tasty bit of prey, the bat will attack them. Since comet moth flight is largely powered by the forewings, if the bat bites off part of a hind wing the moth can still fly well after escaping. The bat loses out, though, with a mouthful of wing instead of the juicy body it was after.

Comet moths are only found in Madagascar.

Moths with longer hind wings have a better chance of escaping bats.

Meanwhile... After a hard day's foraging, the honeybee is tucked up in her cell asleep. It's important she gets at least five hours of sleep. If she doesn't, she will be sluggish and won't be able to forage for nectar and pollen effectively.

Zzzzzzzzzzzzzzzzzzzzzzzzzzn

Glossary

Abdomen
The lower section of an insect body. The abdomen contains the gut, reproductive organs, and anus.

Aggregation
A gathering of insects.

Antennae
A pair of long feelers on the head of an insect.

Arachnids
Eight-legged animals with fangs but no internal backbone. Arachnids belong to a group called invertebrates. Spiders and scorpions are arachnids.

Camouflage
The ability of an animal or plant to blend into its environment to avoid being spotted.

Cocoon
A structure produced by butterflies and moths, inside which the caterpillar can turn into its adult form.

Colony
A group of animals from one species who live close together. Ants and termites live in colonies.

Elytra
Two wing cases that cover the hind wings of a beetle.

Entomologist
A person who studies insects and arachnids.

Fungus
Spore-producing organisms that feed on natural material.

Insects
Six-legged animals that lack internal backbones. Insects belong to a group called invertebrates.

Mandibles
The jaws of an insect.

Metamorphosis
A process of transformation from a juvenile insect stage to the adult form. For example, a caterpillar transforming into a butterfly.

Migration
The seasonal movement of insects (or other animals) across regions.

Nymph
The juvenile stage of insects that do not undergo complete metamorphosis to turn into their adult forms.

Predator
An animal that eats other animals.

Prey
An animal that is eaten by other animals.

Stridulation
The act of making sounds by rubbing body parts together.

Thorax
The insect "torso"—a section of the insect body between the head and the abdomen.

Index

This has been a

NEON SQUID production

I would like to dedicate this book to my grandparents, Harold and Gwen Irons. Thank you also to Aeshna Ware Huff, Zack Ware Huff, and Amelie Ware Redman— junior entomologists extraordinaire!

Author: Dr. Jessica L. Ware
Illustrator: Chaaya Prabhat
US Editor: Allison Singer

Neon Squid would like to thank:
Georgina Coles for proofreading.

Copyright © 2022 St. Martin's Press
120 Broadway, New York, NY 10271

Created for St. Martin's Press
by Neon Squid
The Stables, 4 Crinan Street,
London, N1 9XW

EU representative: Macmillan Publishers Ireland Ltd,
1st Floor, The Liffey Trust Centre,
117-126 Sheriff Street Upper,
Dublin 1, D01 YC43

10 9 8 7 6 5 4 3

The right of Dr. Jessica L. Ware to be identified as the author of this work has been asserted in accordance with the Copyright, Designs and Patents Act, 1988.

All rights reserved. No part of this publication may be reproduced, stored in a retrieval system, or transmitted, in any form or by any means (electronic, mechanical, photocopying, recording or otherwise), without the prior written permission of the publisher.

Library of Congress Cataloging-in-Publication Data is available.

Printed and bound in Guangdong, China by Leo Paper Products Ltd.

ISBN: 978-1-684-49211-4

Published in March 2022.

www.neonsquidbooks.com

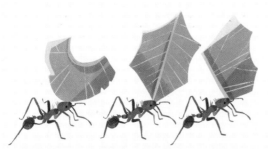